ICONS

History Makers

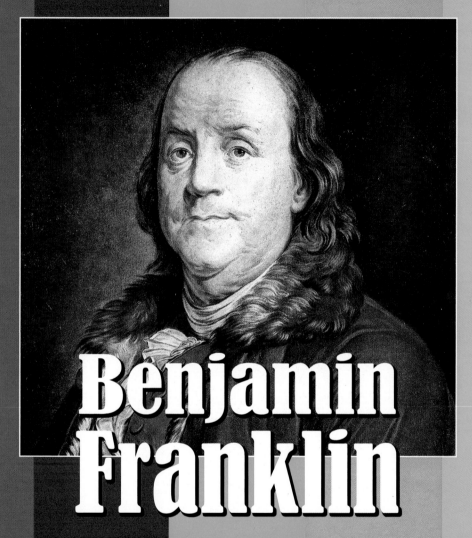

Benjamin Franklin

by Pamela McDowell

www.av2books.com

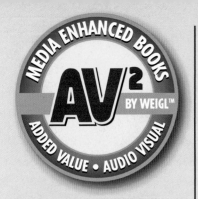

AV² provides enriched content that supplements and complements this book. Weigl's AV² books strive to create inspired learning and engage young minds in a total learning experience.

Your AV² Media Enhanced books come alive with...

Audio
Listen to sections of the book read aloud.

Video
Watch informative video clips.

Embedded Weblinks
Gain additional information for research.

Try This!
Complete activities and hands-on experiments.

Key Words
Study vocabulary, and complete a matching word activity.

Quizzes
Test your knowledge.

Slide Show
View images and captions, and prepare a presentation.

... and much, much more!

Go to **www.av2books.com**, and enter this book's unique code.

BOOK CODE

J 4 1 7 4 7

AV² by Weigl brings you media enhanced books that support active learning.

Published by AV² by Weigl
350 5th Avenue, 59th Floor
New York, NY 10118

www.av2books.com   www.weigl.com

Copyright ©2014 AV² by Weigl

Library of Congress Cataloging-in-Publication Data

McDowell, Pamela.
 Benjamin Franklin / Pamela McDowell.
   p. cm. — (Icons)
 Includes index.
 ISBN 978-1-62127-307-3 (hardcover : alk. paper) —
 ISBN 978-1-62127-313-4 (softcover : alk. paper)
 1. Franklin, Benjamin, 1706-1790—Juvenile literature. 2. Statesmen-United States—Biography—Juvenile literature. 3. Inventors—United States—Biography—Juvenile literature. 4. Scientists—United States—Biography—Juvenile literature. 5. Printers—United States—Biography—Juvenile literature. I. Title.
 E302.6.F8M133 2013
 973.3092—dc23
 [B]
                    2012041283

Printed in the United States of America in North Mankato, Minnesota
1 2 3 4 5 6 7 8 9 0 17 16 15 14 13

WEP040413
052013

Editor: Megan Cuthbert
Design: Terry Paulhus

Photograph Credits
Weigl acknowledges Getty Images as the primary image supplier for this title. Every reasonable effort has been made to trace ownership and to obtain permission to reprint copyright material. The publishers would be pleased to have any errors or omissions brought to their attention so that they may be corrected in subsequent printings.

Contents

Who Was Benjamin Franklin?

Benjamin Franklin is one of the **Founding Fathers** of the United States. He helped the 13 American **colonies** separate from Great Britain. He signed two important documents, the Declaration of Independence and the Constitution. These are the legal documents that created the United States of America.

Benjamin Franklin was a **statesman** and a **diplomat**. He crossed the Atlantic eight times in his work as a representative of the North American colonies. Benjamin was also a scientist, inventor, postmaster, and author. His experiments with electricity and lightning are well-known, and some of his inventions can still be found in houses today. Swim fins, bifocal glasses, and the Franklin stove are a few of his useful inventions.

Before all this, Benjamin Franklin was a successful printer. His letters, newspapers and books helped him share his ideas with the colonists.

"If you would not be forgotten as soon as you are dead and rotten, either write things worth reading or do things worth the writing."

Growing Up

Benjamin Franklin was born on January 17, 1706, in Boston, Massachusetts. Benjamin's father, Josiah, was a tradesman who made candles and soaps. Shortly after the death of his first wife, Josiah married Benjamin's mother, Abiah. The two were not wealthy and worked hard to support 17 children.

Benjamin was a quick learner. Josiah and Abiah hoped that he might become a preacher. They sent him to Boston Latin School, where he rose to the head of his class. This formal education was expensive, so Josiah took his son out of Boston Latin School and sent him to a regular school. After two years of writing and arithmetic, Josiah decided Benjamin had learned enough. He put the 10-year-old boy to work with him.

Making candles from animal fat was smelly and boring. Benjamin grew unhappy with the work. In the 1700s, it was normal for a son to learn the family trade and then start his own business. Benjamin did not look forward to this future. He wanted to be challenged and to share his ideas. He did not want to make candles and soap for the rest of his life.

▲ Benjamin Franklin was the youngest son in the Franklin family. His father had seven children with his first wife, Anne, and ten children with his second wife, Abiah.

Get to Know
Massachusetts

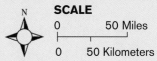

NEW
HAMPSHIRE

VERMONT

MASSACHUSETTS

RHODE
ISLAND

NEW
YORK

CONNECTICUT

ATLANTIC
OCEAN

SCALE

N

0   50 Miles

0   50 Kilometers

The Mayflower was the ship that brought the first settlers from Great Britain to Massachusetts in 1620.

The state capital of Massachusetts is Boston. About 625,000 people live in the city of Boston.

Massachusetts is one of the New England states. These are the states where British people first settled in North America.

Cape Cod is a popular tourism destination in Massachusetts. It is a peninsula where visitors enjoy fishing, whale watching, and sailing.

STATE SYMBOLS

TREE
American Elm

BIRD
Chickadee

FLOWER
Mayflower

Practice Makes Perfect

Josiah understood that Benjamin would not be satisfied making soaps and candles. When he was 12, Benjamin was **apprenticed** to his older brother, James, who was a Boston printer. Benjamin was contracted to work for James as an apprentice until he was 21, learning the trade and receiving meals, clothes, and a place to live instead of pay.

Printing was a challenging trade. Each page of printed material was made separately by placing every letter of every word on a metal plate. This had to be done backwards, from right to left, so the page printed correctly when it was placed on the printing press. Benjamin mastered this task. He hoped to write for the newspaper, but James refused. Benjamin decided to write anyway. He submitted his writing under the name 'Silence Dogood.' James became angry when he discovered he had been tricked into printing Benjamin's letters. The letters became popular with readers. James' anger and jealousy grew.

◄ James printed two of Benjamin's poems, which Benjamin sold in the city.

At 17, Benjamin ran away. He found work in Philadelphia and eventually opened his own print shop, producing government pamphlets, books, and money. He started publishing a newspaper called the *Pennsylvania Gazette* in 1729. When there were not enough letters or articles to fill the paper, Benjamin wrote them himself using made-up names.

Benjamin Franklin's first major success as a writer and printer came in 1732, when he published *Poor Richard's Almanack*. This book was a collection of witty sayings, poems, calendars, practical advice, and **proverbs**. It became so popular that he continued to write and publish it for 25 years.

QUICK FACTS

- Benjamin published America's first political cartoon.
- Young Benjamin became an excellent swimmer and invented fins to help him swim faster.
- At 16, Benjamin read a book about vegetable diets and became a vegetarian.

◀ Almanacks were a popular form of entertainment that included weather forecasts, household tips, and puzzles.

Key Events

Benjamin became known throughout the Pennsylvania colony for his printing business and his contributions to the community. He used his influence and money to found the colony's first lending library, its first police patrol, and a volunteer fire company, as well as many other services. He was a very respected member of the colony.

By the late 1740s, Benjamin was ready for new challenges. He retired from his printing business to explore other interests. During this time, he began conducting science experiments. He used his discoveries to create useful objects. One of his first creations was the lightning rod. This metal rod was attached to the top of a building. When lightning struck the rod, its electricity ran down a wire into the ground instead of causing a fire or damaging the building.

Benjamin was also very interested in politics. In 1751, he was elected to the Pennsylvania Assembly. The assembly was created to be the colony's government. In reality, however, it had little power. Benjamin wanted to see the colony become more **autonomous**. He began talking to people in the other colonies about becoming more independent. In 1757, he traveled to Great Britain as the colony's representative.

◀ Benjamin proved that lightning was electricity by flying a kite with a key attached to it during a lightning storm. He used the knowledge he gained from the experiment to help create the lightning rod.

Thoughts from Benjamin

Benjamin Franklin had many roles in his life. Here are some of his comments on his broad range of interests.

Benjamin explains why he never defended his opinions.
"I leave them to take their chance in the world. If they are *right*, truth and experience will support them; if *wrong*, they ought to be refuted and rejected."

Benjamin talks about why he did not patent his inventions.
"As we enjoy great advantages from the inventions of others, we should be glad of an opportunity to serve others by any invention of ours; and this we should do freely and generously."

Benjamin's views on learning something new.
"Tell me and I forget. Teach me and I remember. Involve me and I learn."

Benjamin talks about the national bird.
"For my own part I wish the Bald Eagle had not been chosen the Representative of our Country....the Turkey is in Comparison a much more respectable Bird, and withal a true original Native of America."

Benjamin comments on the risk of signing the Declaration of Independence.
"We must all hang together, or most assuredly we will all hang separately."

Some of Benjamin's sayings from *Poor Richard's Almanack* are still used today.
"A penny saved is a penny earned."

What Is an Inventor?

An inventor is a person who creates something new. An inventor is curious and is looking for a better way to do something. Inventors often form **partnerships**. Each person in the partnership brings different skills and strengths to the project. Together, they can create things that they might not achieve on their own.

An inventor experiments using trial and error. This means that he or she must test ideas many times and expect to make mistakes. Much can be learned from these mistakes. Benjamin experimented with electricity for many years before he successfully created the lightning rod.

New words are often created with a new invention. The words "battery," "charge," "condenser," and "conductor" are some of the words Benjamin created to describe parts of his electricity experiments and inventions. These are words commonly used today.

▲ Benjamin performed many experiments with electricity. He discovered that two objects that had the same electrical charge would repel each other.

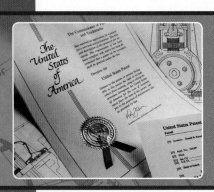

WHAT IS A PATENT?

Inventors often choose to patent their discoveries. The person who owns the patent has exclusive rights to make, use, and sell the invention. The patent is granted by the government for a period of time, usually 20 years. A patent protects an inventor's idea. In some countries, ignoring a patent and using the inventor's idea is illegal.

Inventors 101

Alexander Graham Bell (1847–1922)

Alexander Graham Bell was born in Edinburgh, Scotland. He built his first invention when he was 12 years old. In 1871, Bell moved to Boston, where he formed a partnership with an electrician named Thomas Watson. Together, they developed the telephone. Alexander demonstrated the invention at the Centennial Exhibition in Pennsylvania in 1876. He became known around the world as an inventor.

Thomas Edison (1847–1931)

Thomas Edison grew up in Michigan. He was a great reader but a difficult student. At 15, he was employed as a telegraph operator, but this became difficult as he lost his hearing. He developed and sold his first invention, an improved stock ticker, for $40,000. He went on to develop the phonograph, an improved light bulb, and a longer-lasting battery. Thomas held 1,093 patents in the U.S. during his lifetime.

Lonnie G. Johnson (1949–)

Lonnie G. Johnson was born in Mobile, Alabama. His father encouraged him to build his own toys. When he was 13, Johnson powered a go-kart with a lawnmower engine. Lonnie went on to earn university degrees in engineering. He joined the Air Force, where he helped develop the stealth bomber program. The program designed aircraft that are undetectable by sensors. Lonnie was creating an environmentally friendly heat pump when he discovered he had made a powerful water gun. He patented the Super Soaker, which remains one of the most popular toys in the world.

Steve Jobs (1955–2011)

Steve Jobs grew up in Mountain View, California, in an area known as the Silicon Valley. His father taught him to take things apart and rebuild them. In 1976, Steve started Apple Computers with his friend, computer engineer Steve Wozniak. The pair wanted to develop personal computers that were easy to use. Today, Apple continues to create new products such as the iPod, iPad, and iPhone.

Influences

One of the few books Benjamin's family owned was Cotton Mather's book *Bonifacius, or Essays to Do Good*. This book talked about ways to help society. The ideas expressed in the book taught young Benjamin about **community service**. Throughout his life, Benjamin worked hard, not just to become wealthy, but to improve life in the colonies.

Benjamin loved reading and hoped to be like the writers he admired. He read and reread the work of Richard Addison and Joseph Steele, who founded the newspaper *The Spectator*. He learned a sense of style from these writers and went on to develop his own style of writing.

▲ Benjamin co-founded the Pennsylvania Hospital in 1751 to help the sick and poor of Philadelphia. The first patients were admitted to the hospital in 1756.

Benjamin met famous scientists and authors in his travels to England and France. Later in his life, he worked with other Founding Fathers, including George Washington, John Adams, Thomas Jefferson, John Jay, Alexander Hamilton, and James Madison. Talking and sharing ideas with these men helped strengthen his belief in independence for the colonies.

THE FRANKLIN FAMILY

Benjamin Franklin lived in Philadelphia, Pennsylvania, with his wife, Deborah, son, William, and daughter, Sarah. Another son, Francis, died of smallpox when he was four years old. Over time, Sarah had seven children who often visited their grandparents. Two grandsons even accompanied Benjamin on a mission to Paris.

▲ Benjamin's work often kept him away from his family. Although Benjamin did not see his wife Deborah for long periods of time, they wrote each other regularly.

Overcoming Obstacles

Benjamin was proud of his **working-class** roots. With 16 brothers and sisters, young Benjamin learned to fend for himself. He never forgot the hard work and determination it took for him to rise from poverty.

▲ Colonists were growing frustrated with the British control of goods for the colonies. On June 9, 1772, a group of Rhode Island citizens sunk the Gaspee, a British customs ship.

▲ The colonists did not want to pay the high tax on British tea. When ships carrying tea arrived in Boston harbor, a group boarded the ships and dumped the tea into the harbor in protest.

One of Benjamin's greatest challenges was trying to create peaceful independence for the 13 colonies. When the Pennsylvania colony sent Benjamin to Great Britain in 1757, he was to fight for fair **taxes**. The colony's citizens were paying large amounts of money in taxes to the British government. The Penn family, the colony's owners, did not have to pay any taxes. Benjamin argued that the Penn family should have to pay taxes as well. The British **Parliament** did not care about laws that affected the colonies. This frustrated Benjamin. He returned to Pennsylvania in 1762.

Pennsylvania and the other colonies continued to struggle with their lack of freedom and the taxes they were required to pay. Benjamin traveled to Great Britain again in 1764. This time, his goal was to convince King George III that the colonies would run better if they were allowed to govern themselves. He stayed there for the next 11 years, trying to convince the British government to change the laws. He did not succeed. When he returned to Pennsylvania in 1775, he recommended that the colonies separate from Great Britain.

Achievements and Successes

In 1776, Benjamin worked alongside Thomas Jefferson, John Adams, Robert Livingston, and Roger Sherman to **draft** the Declaration of Independence. The document helped justify the colony's ongoing battles with British forces. On July 4, 1776, the Declaration of Independence was signed, and the 13 American colonies declared their freedom from British rule.

The American Revolutionary War was not easy for the newly created United States of America. As colonies, they had depended on Great Britain. Now, they had to find new ways to get the resources they needed. Benjamin traveled to France to see if its government would help the United States in the war effort. He asked France to provide soldiers, supplies, and money. The French agreed and became allies of the new country. Later, Benjamin traveled to France to help **negotiate** and draft the 1783 Treaty of Paris. This treaty ended the war.

▲ **In 1778, Benjamin signed the Treaty of Alliance with the French government. He was well-liked by the French court, and he became the first ever U.S. Ambassador to France.**

After the war, Benjamin was concerned that the states would break apart. He believed that a constitution would help keep them united. Benjamin returned to Philadelphia, and joined the Constitutional Convention in 1787. This meeting resulted in the creation of the U.S. Constitution.

Benjamin died in Philadelphia in 1790. More than 20,000 people attended his funeral. He remains one of the most important people in American history.

PAYING TRIBUTE TO BENJAMIN FRANKLIN

Benjamin Franklin spent many years working to improve living conditions in the colonies. His efforts helped to create the free country Americans enjoy today. There are about 5,000 likenesses of Benjamin Franklin within the city of Philadelphia. His name has been used all over the country, including the Benjamin Franklin Bridge over the Delaware River, several U.S. Navy ships, and counties in at least 16 U.S. states. His image has appeared on the $100 dollar bill since 1928.

A statue of Benjamin Franklin stands outside the Old Post Office Pavilion in Washington D.C. Benjamin served as Deputy Postmaster General of North America for 20 years and helped improve the U.S. Postal system.

Write a Biography

A person's life story can be the subject of a book. This kind of book is called a biography. Biographies describe the lives of remarkable people, such as those who have achieved great success or have done important things to help others. These people may be alive today, or they may have lived many years ago. Reading a biography can help you learn more about a remarkable person.

At school, you might be asked to write a biography. First, decide who you want to write about. You can choose an inventor, such as Benjamin Franklin, or any other person. Then, find out if your library has any books about this person.

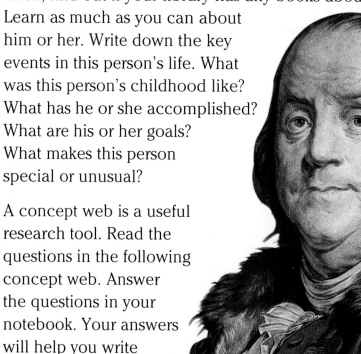

Learn as much as you can about him or her. Write down the key events in this person's life. What was this person's childhood like? What has he or she accomplished? What are his or her goals? What makes this person special or unusual?

A concept web is a useful research tool. Read the questions in the following concept web. Answer the questions in your notebook. Your answers will help you write a biography.

Your Opinion

- What did you learn from the books you read in your research?
- Would you suggest these books to others?
- Was anything missing from these books?

Childhood

- Where and when was this person born?
- Describe his or her parents, siblings, and friends.
- Did this person grow up in unusual circumstances?

Adulthood

- Where does this individual currently reside?
- Does he or she have a family?

Writing a Biography

Main Accomplishments

- What is this person's life's work?
- Has he or she received awards or recognition for accomplishments?
- How have this person's accomplishments served others?

Work and Preparation

- What was this person's education?
- What was his or her work experience?
- How does this person work; what is or was the process he or she uses or used?

Help and Obstacles

- Did this individual have a positive attitude?
- Did he or she receive help from others?
- Did this person have a mentor?
- Did this person face any hardships?
- If so, how were the hardships overcome?

Timeline

YEAR	BENJAMIN FRANKLIN	WORLD EVENTS
1706	Benjamin Franklin is born on January 17.	French and Spanish soldiers unsuccessfully attack Charleston, South Carolina, in an attempt to capture it from the British.
1732	The first edition of *Poor Richard's Almanack* is published.	George Washington is born.
1743	Benjamin helps found the Pennsylvania Academy and College.	Thomas Jefferson is born.
1752	Benjamin conducts his kite experiment.	The first hospital in the colonies opens its doors in Pennsylvania.
1761	Benjamin invents the **glass armonica**.	King George III of Great Britain is officially crowned king at his coronation ceremony.
1776	Benjamin signs the Declaration of Independence.	British troops evacuate Boston after the city is surrounded by American troops.
1790	Benjamin Franklin dies.	George Washington gives his first State of the Union address as the country's first president.

Key Words

apprenticed: sent to learn a trade from an experienced person

autonomous: not controlled by others, acting independently

colonies: areas that are ruled by a more powerful country

community service: working to help other people

diplomat: a person who handles relations between his or her country and other countries

draft: to draw or write a plan

Founding Fathers: the political leaders who helped form the United States

glass armonica: a musical instrument made of different-sized glass bowls

negotiate: to bargain or deal with someone to try to find a solution

parliament: a group of people who make the laws of a country

partnerships: when two or more people join together, usually for business

patent: to obtain the right to be the only one to make, use, or sell an invention

proverbs: short sayings that express thoughts many people believe to be true

statesman: a person who helps to guide important issues and government

taxes: money paid to the government for goods or services

treaty: a formal agreement between countries or people

working-class: people who work at lower-paying jobs

Index

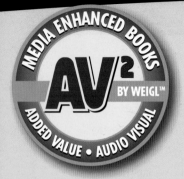

Log on to www.av2books.com

AV² by Weigl brings you media enhanced books that support active learning. Go to www.av2books.com, and enter the special code found on page 2 of this book. You will gain access to enriched and enhanced content that supplements and complements this book. Content includes video, audio, weblinks, quizzes, a slide show, and activities.

AV² Online Navigation

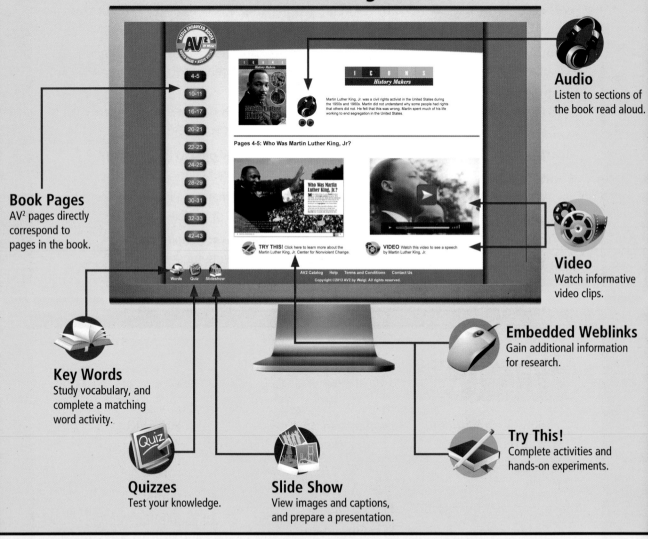

Book Pages
AV² pages directly correspond to pages in the book.

Audio
Listen to sections of the book read aloud.

Video
Watch informative video clips.

Embedded Weblinks
Gain additional information for research.

Try This!
Complete activities and hands-on experiments.

Key Words
Study vocabulary, and complete a matching word activity.

Quizzes
Test your knowledge.

Slide Show
View images and captions, and prepare a presentation.

AV² was built to bridge the gap between print and digital. We encourage you to tell us what you like and what you want to see in the future.

Sign up to be an AV² Ambassador at www.av2books.com/ambassador.